The Bag Family

Printed in the United States of America

First Printing, 2018

ISBN-13: 978-0-692-15136-5 (Hardcover edition)

Editor: Tonia Jenny www.ToniaJenny.com

Published by the authors
TheBagFamilyBook@gmail.com

The Bag Family

By Karen Zander
Illustrated by Dawn Nelson

Dedicated to the many forms
of families in our world.

The big pink bag sat in the hallway by the front door. She thought of mom, dad, and brother who had brought her here with baby sister earlier today. The family had gone to bed and she was lonely.

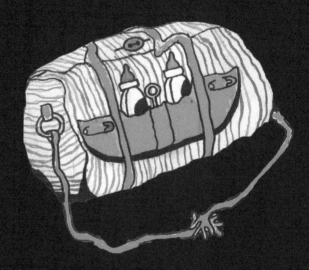

As the house grew darker, she began to cry. Big tears flowed from her eyes.

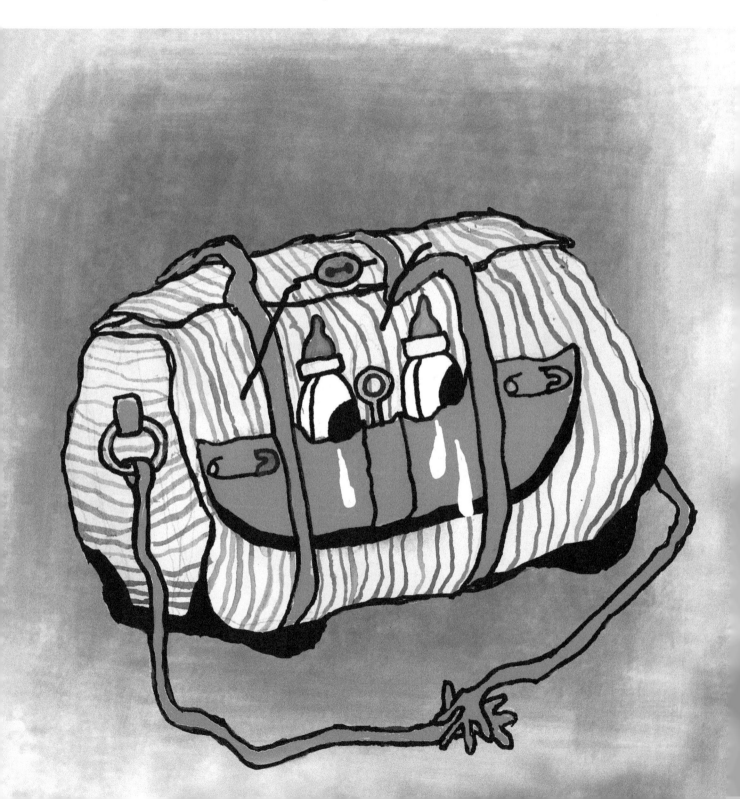

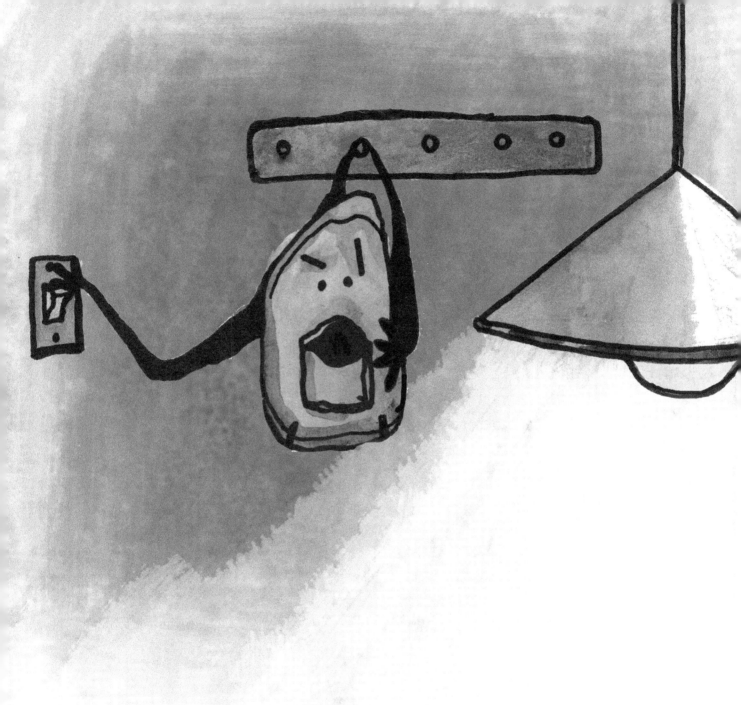

"Hey, what's wrong?" came a voice from the dark.
The voice belonged to a blue backpack in the kitchen.
He switched on the light. "Hi! I'm Benji," he said. "Who
are you?"

"Gee, I don't have a name."

"We all have names here. Hi! I'm Dumpy. I hold the garbage. We talk at night while the family sleeps. During the day, we are busy!"

"Yes, we are! I'm Mom's purse, and she needs me for everything! May we call you Stripey?"

"I'm Pricilla. I live where Mom leaves me last, which is usually on the kitchen table. You have already met Dumpy and Benji."

"Let me introduce you to Duffy and the Baggies, who live on the kitchen shelves above Dumpy. Duffy carries Dad's gym clothes."

"Dad packs lunches for everyone in the Baggies."

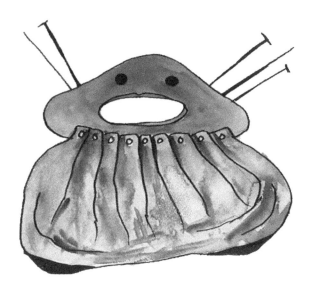

A quiet voice came from the living room. "I am Nedeelia, Grandma's knitting bag. I came here with Grandma today to help with the new baby."

"HEY! You forgot about me, just like Aunt Audrey did! She just dropped me here on the floor by the back door when she came in from work. I carry a heavy load. I am Ms. Brief, and all I want to do is to be appreciated!"

"We are the bags the family uses every day." explained Benji.

Meanwhile, Peppy, the family pet, heard the noise and came downstairs. He was always very curious.

Peppy found Stripey at the bottom of the stairs, and took out one of her bottles.

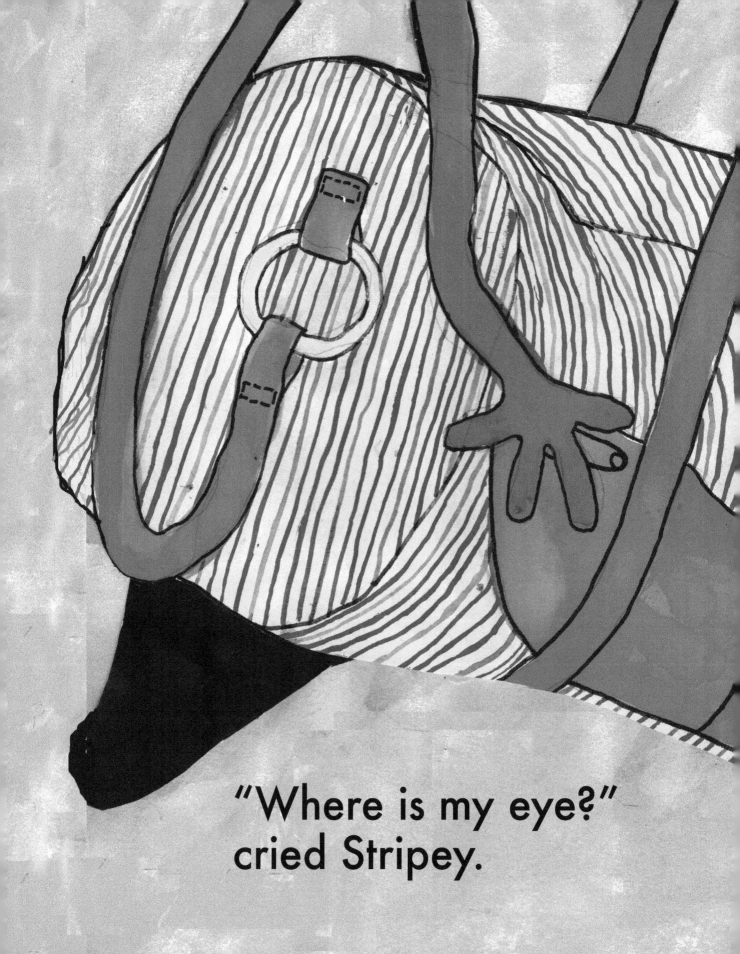

"Where is my eye?"
cried Stripey.

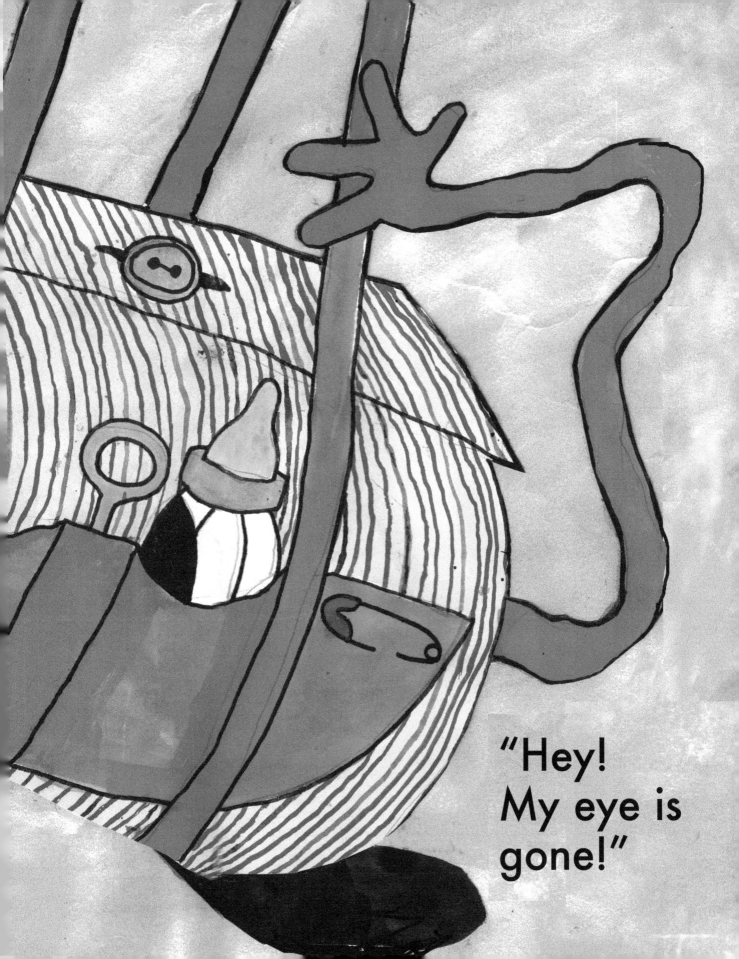

Benji saw Peppy with Stripey's eye. He got an idea. "Let's switch what is in all of the bags and see what happens," he said.

Ha HA HA Ha Ha

"Maybe THIS will get Aunt Audrey's attention!"
Ms. Brief laughed.

So Peppy got to work. He brought a bottle
and the diapers to Benji to carry.

It took two full bags to carry what was in Ms. Brief!
Peppy took the laptop to Nedeelia, and the legal
briefs and computer mouse to Stripey. Then, Peppy
moved the wallet, keys, and glasses from Pricilla to
Ms. Brief. Now Ms. Brief was very light.

Peppy moved Nedeelia's
yarn and knitting needles
to the Baggies...

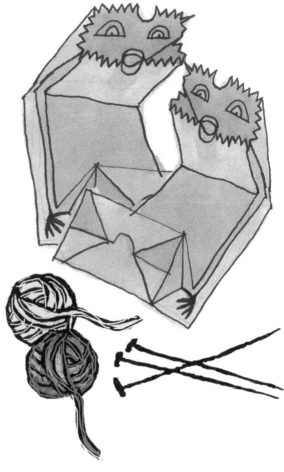

Dad's gym shoes
from Duffy to
Dumpy...

And finally moved the soggy corncob, the apple core, empty milk carton, and open can of peas to Pricilla.

All of the bags seemed to have fun with the switches of their favorite items.

(X-ray photo)

After everything was switched around...

...everyone fell asleep,

except for Stripey.
She kept thinking,
"What will happen
tomorrow?"

At school, Brother pulled out the bottle and the diapers.

The kids laughed and called him a big baby!

When Mom went to run an errand, she found garbage in Pricilla . . .

Grandma tried to pick up Nedeelia, who was so heavy that Grandma fell back in her chair and couldn't get up.

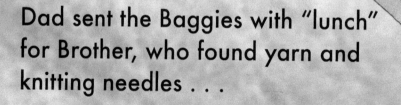

Dad sent the Baggies with "lunch" for Brother, who found yarn and knitting needles . . .

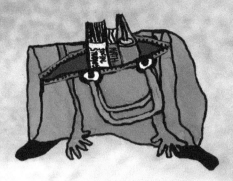

Dad got to the gym and had books in his gym bag, so he couldn't work out.

? instead of her keys.

Mom told Dad that she had found his sneakers in Dumpy.

instead of his lunch.

And lastly, Ms. Brief, who only wanted Aunt Audrey to appreciate her, was so sad because Aunt Audrey didn't go to work today, and never even noticed.

Later that night, all the bags were talking at once,

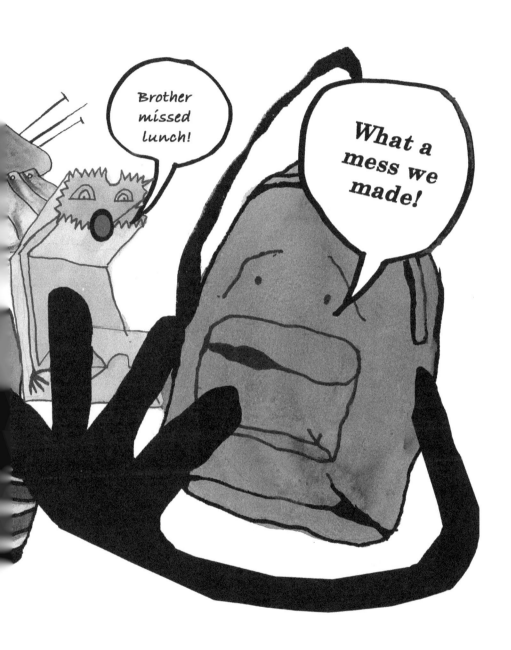

until Benji said, "What a mess we made!"

Benji thought about what happened and said, "It wasn't a very good idea. We thought it would be funny, but it upset everyone. Let's put everything back where it belongs, and NOT do this again!"

All the bags agreed!

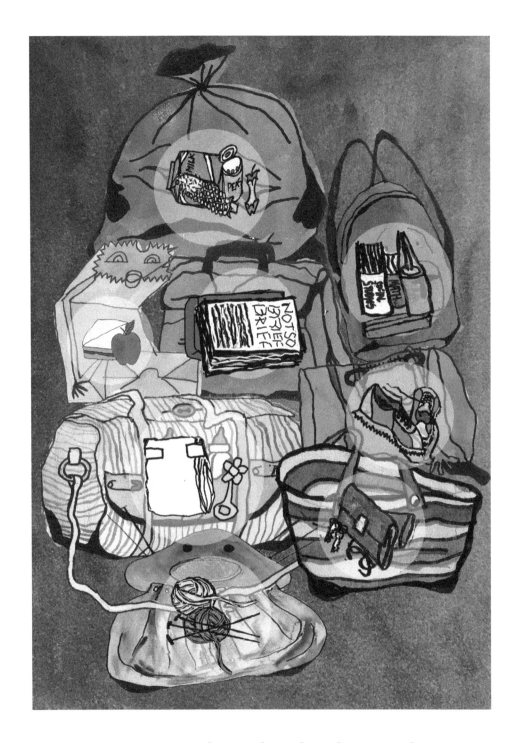

Peppy put everything back where it belonged, and everyone felt much better.

Nedeelia, being the oldest and wisest bag, said, "We each have an important job to do, and each of us is different—just like the family we live with. Ms. Brief, Aunt Audrey may not appreciate the weight you carry, but we sure do! And Stripey, you are a very wonderful addition to our family! I don't think we ever realized it before, but we are a family too!"

The Bag Family

Thank you...

Thanks to everyone who has helped us over the years to transform this idea into a book, and special thanks to Bernie, Dez, Elise, Victoria, Sue, Elizabeth, Vin, Betty, Sue, Andrew, Linda, Opie, Kate, Shelley, Suzanne and Tonia for your help, encouragement, and support!

The Storytellers

Karen Zander (writer) and Dawn Nelson (illustrator) met as students at Illinois Wesleyan University in 1969. Both moved to Boston for their careers after college, Karen as a nurse and Dawn as an art teacher.

In the 1980s, they got the idea to create a children's book together. Amidst their busy lives, they came up with the story idea and the characters for "The Bag Family." But before they were able to finish the project, their own bags overflowed with work, life and family commitments. Three decades later, as they neared retirement, they revisited their old bag—literally. Dawn had stored the original story, art and papers in an old bag in the back of her closet. So, they finally completed the book together! Karen and Dawn are overjoyed to have brought this story to life, and they hope you love "The Bag Family!"

CPSIA information can be obtained
at www.ICGtesting.com
Printed in the USA
BVHW02*0937030918
526184BV00008B/7/P